A ROOKIE READER®

BRAVE MARY

By Larry Dane Brimner

Illustrations by Marilyn Mets

℗ Children's Press®
A Division of Grolier Publishing
New York   London   Hong Kong   Sydney
Danbury, Connecticut

For Judy Enderle and Stephanie Tessler

Library of Congress Cataloging–in–Publication Data

Brimner, Larry Dane.
   Brave Mary/Larry Dane Brimner; illustrations by Marilyn Mets.
      p. cm. — (A rookie reader)
   Summary: Everyone says Mary is brave, as she performs a number
of tasks that require courage.
   ISBN 0-516-02056-0
   [1. Courage—Fiction. 2. Stories in rhyme.] I. Mets, Marilyn, ill.
II. Title. III Series.

PZ8.3.B77145Br 1996   95-43500
[E]—dc20   CIP
                                   AC

Everybody says Mary is brave.

Her brother.

The teacher.

Her mother.

The preacher.

No matter when.
No matter what.

Brave Mary is brave.
Tut-tut! Tut-tut!

She sleeps alone in the attic.
And swims in the lake.

She answers hard questions.
And feeds the class snake.

A knock on the door?
A thump on the stair?

A cat in the tower?
Brave Mary's there.

Saving the hour.

Saving the day.

Brave Mary is brave.

Hip-hip!
    Hooray!

About the Author

Larry Dane Brimner, a native of Florida, grew up in Alaska and California. A teacher for twenty years, he is now the author of more than thirty fiction and nonfiction books for young people. When he isn't writing, he visits elementary schools throughout the country to discuss the writing process with young authors and readers. He relaxes by gardening, reading a good mystery, or taking a spin on his mountain bike in Colorado's San Juan Mountains.

About the Artist

Marilyn Mets studied in Canada at Ontario College of Art, Toronto, and Sheridan College, Oakville. Early in her career, she worked in promotion illustration and design for the *Toronto Star*. For the past several years, she has concentrated on illustrating children's books and painting for pleasure — while balancing babies, diapers, numerous children, wild animals, and the kitchen sink on one knee!

Along with book illustration, Marilyn is also working for *Today's Parent* magazine. On her days off, she can usually be found giggling in the children's section of the local library. She lives in Toronto, Ontario, with her three children, two frogs, and one husband.